D1358340

Some of the animations accompanying this book incude toolbars. Here's how to use the most common buttons.

Tap this to reset the app to the beginning.

Tap this to show/hide the icon bar.

Tap this to restart the app.

Tap this to take a picture.

Use these to navigate.

Need some help?
If you've got a problem, check out our website:

www.carltonbooks.co.uk/icarltonbooks/help

From the Exhibition Department at the American Museum of Natural History:
Creative Direction: David Harvey, Lauri Halderman, Helene Alonso
Writing & Editorial: Eliza McCarthy, Martin Schwabacher, Sasha Nemecek
Interaction & Modeling: Harry Borrelli, Camila Engelbert, Erin Arden, Kim Raichstat
Project Management: Betina Cochran, Alex Navissi
This book was produced in conjunction with the exhibition *Beyond Planet Earth: The Future of Space Exploration*, created by the American Museum of Natural History and curated by Michael Shara.

THIS IS A CARLTON BOOK

Text, design and illustration:
© Carlton Books Limited 2013
Beyond Planet Earth Exhibition: The Future of Space Exploration:
© 2013 American Museum of Natural History

Published in 2013 by Carlton Books Limited.
An imprint of the Carlton Publishing Group,
20 Mortimer Street, London, W1T 3JW.

A catalogue record for this book is available from the British Library.

ISBN: 978-1-78312-080-2
Printed in China

The American Museum of Natural History in New York City is one of the largest and most respected museums in the world. Since the Museum was founded in 1869, its collections have grown to include more than 32 million specimens and artifacts relating to the natural world and human cultures. The Museum showcases its collections in the exhibit halls, and, behind the scenes, more than 200 scientists carry out cutting-edge research. It is also home to the Theodore Roosevelt Memorial, New York State's official memorial to its 33rd governor and the nation's 26th president, and a tribute to Roosevelt's enduring legacy of conservation. Approximately 5 million people from around the world visit the Museum each year. Plan a trip to the Museum, home of the world's largest collection of dinosaur fossils, or visit online at www.amnh.org.

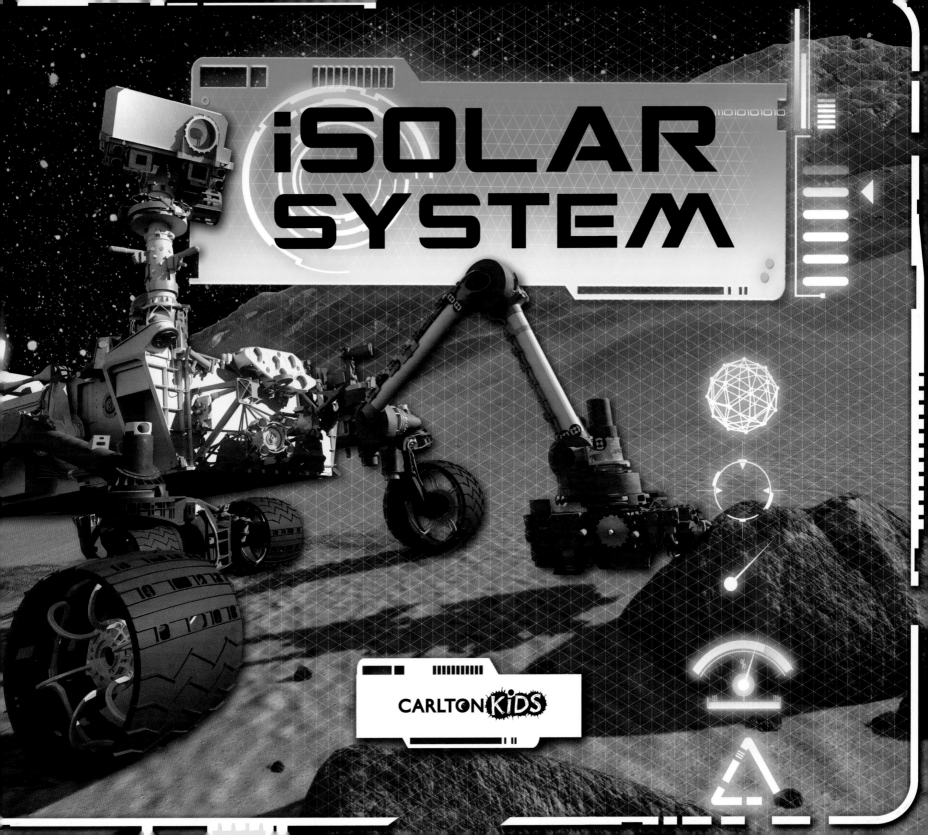

OUR SOLAR SYSTEM

Our solar system contains just one star – the Sun – with eight planets, millions of rocky asteroids, icy comets and dwarf planets, including Pluto, in orbit around it. So far, humans have only set foot on our own Moon, so there is a lot left to explore.

THE EIGHT PLANETS

How Big and How Far?
The graphic below shows the relative sizes of the eight planets in our solar system, compared to the Sun. What isn't shown is the relative distance between the planets. This is because, to do that, you would need a page the size of a football field! The four outer planets are much farther away than the four inner planets.

THE SUN

Mass: 333,000 Earths
Composition: 92.1% Hydrogen, 7.8% Helium, 0.1% other elements
Surface gravity: About 28 times that at Earth's surface

▲ MERCURY
Average distance from Sun: 36 million miles (58 million km)
Moons: None
Mass: 0.055 Earths
Orbital period: nearly 88 days
Named after: the Roman god of trade

▲ VENUS
Average distance from Sun: 67 million miles (108 million km)
Moons: None
Mass: 0.815 Earths
Orbital period: 224.7 days
Named after: the Roman goddess of love and beauty

▲ EARTH
Average distance from Sun: 93 million miles (150 million km)
Moons: One
Orbital period: 365 days

▲ MARS
Average distance from Sun: 142 million miles (228 million km)
Moons: Two
Mass: 0.1 Earths
Orbital period: 687 days
Named after: the Roman god of war

AUGMENTED REALITY

Tap the planet icons to see each one in close-up, then tap the Sun to view the whole system again. Use the slider bar to increase or decrease the planets' rotation speed. The counter tells you how many times Earth has gone around the Sun (marking a year) since you started watching.

PLUTO, THE DWARF PLANET

Pluto is no longer considered a planet in the technical sense, since it is too small to clear other objects from its orbital path. It is now called a "dwarf planet". Icy Pluto, along with its five moons, including Charon, is located in the Kuiper Belt, an area billions of miles from the Sun that contains at least 100,000 other orbiting objects.

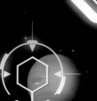

▲ JUPITER

Average distance from Sun: 484 million miles (778 million km)
Moons: at least 64
Mass: 318 Earths
Orbital period: 11.9 years
Named after: the Roman king of the gods

▲ SATURN

Average distance from Sun: 886 million miles (1.4 billion km)
Moons: at least 53
Mass: 95 Earths
Orbital period: 29.5 years
Named after: the Roman god of agriculture

▲ URANUS

Average distance from Sun: 1.8 billion miles (2.9 billion km)
Moons: at least 27
Mass: 14.5 Earths
Orbital period: 84 years
Discovered: 1781
Named after: the Ancient Greek god of the sky

▲ NEPTUNE

Average distance from Sun: 2.8 billion miles (4.5 billion km)
Moons: 13
Mass: 17.1 Earths
Orbital period: 164.8 years
Discovered: 1846
Named after: the Roman god of the sea

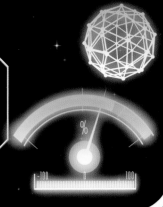

◉ *Planetary Rings*
The four outer planets – Jupiter, Saturn, Uranus and Neptune – all have rings. Saturn has the most, and the widest (shown here). They measure 180,000 miles (290,000 km) from one side to the other.

RACE TO THE MOON

⊙ Apollo 11 Lunar Module
Known as the Eagle, this craft landed on the Moon on July 20, 1969.

In the twentieth century, a race began between the USA and the Soviet Union (a country that included modern-day Russia) to see who would be the first to land on the Moon. In 1969, the USA succeeeded. 12 American men – but no women – walked on the Moon between 1969 and 1972.

THE MOON

VITAL STATISTICS
17% Earth's gravity
29.5 days to orbit Earth
2,160 miles (3,475 km) in diameter, about 27% that of Earth

DISTANCE FROM EARTH
238,857 miles/384,400 km (average)
135 days by car at 70 mph (113 km/h)
3 days on Apollo 11

⊙ Versatile Vehicle
The Eagle was designed to land on the Moon and then be able to carry astronauts back up into orbit.

AUGMENTED REALITY

Use pinch, swipe, and zoom to explore the bare, rocky surface of the Moon. Earth's satellite has no atmosphere, so asteroids drawn in by its gravity smash straight into its surface, leaving huge craters.

SPACE RACE TIMELINE

1957
The Soviet Union launches Sputnik, the first artificial satellite ever to orbit Earth.

1959
Luna 2, the first probe on the Moon, is landed by the Soviet Union.

1961
Russian Yuri Gagarin becomes the first man in space.

1963
Russian Valentina Tereshkova becomes the first woman in space.

1968
The USA's manned Apollo 8 mission successfully orbits the Moon.

1969
The Apollo 11 mission lands Americans Buzz Aldrin and Neil Armstrong on the surface of the Moon.

WALKING ON THE MOON

The USA, motivated by the Soviet successes of the late 1950s and early 1960s, worked hard to send humans to the Moon. They made it on July 20, 1969, when two men walked on the lunar surface, watched by a TV audience of 600 million people. Buzz Aldrin and Neil Armstrong spent 12 hours there, hopping around in the low gravity and collecting lunar rocks for study.

THE FIRST MAN IN SPACE

On April 12, 1961, Soviet astronaut Yuri Gagarin became the first person in space. Gagarin orbited the planet once, during an 108-minute flight in the Vostok 1 capsule.
"I see Earth!" he said from space. "It is so beautiful." He landed back on Earth by ejecting from the capsule and parachuting to the ground.

THINGS GO WRONG

Apollo 13 was to be the third mission to land on the Moon, but never made it. Instead, an explosion in one of the oxygen tanks cut electrical power and oxygen supply to part of the craft. The astronauts were forced just to orbit the Moon, instead of landing. The famous line "Houston, we have a problem" is a quotation from astronaut Jack Swigert during this mission.

> "That's one small step for man; one giant leap for mankind."
>
> Neil Armstrong, Apollo 11 commander

A BASE ON THE MOON

Nobody has visited the Moon since 1972. Today, many scientists and engineers around the world are determined to send people back there.

AUGMENTED REALITY

Move your device to look around this model of a Bigelow base. Inflatable modules like these could serve as both spacecraft and static base components.

WHERE TO LAND?

Shackleton Crater near the Moon's south pole is one of the most likely destinations. The region has ice probably left over from comet impacts, plus sunlight on crater rims and plenty of dirt that could help humans "live off the land" there someday.

ALL-PURPOSE MODULES

Launching heavy, rocket-powered spacecraft from Earth is extremely expensive. Expandable modules, made with walls of reinforced fabric, could be used for the living areas of spaceships and also to construct a base on the surface of the Moon. Three of these modules could provide nearly as much living space as some houses. By contrast, the Apollo lunar modules were about the size of a jail cell.

SHACKLETON CRATER

VITAL STATISTICS
Depth: 2.5 miles (4km)
Width: 12 miles (20km)
Rim temperature: about –100F (–73C)
Bottom temperature: about –351F (–213C)
Named after: Ernest Shackleton (1874-1922), the British Antarctic explorer.

RESOURCES

Oxygen: Tanks of liquid oxygen would be brought from Earth, for astronauts to breathe and for rocket fuel. Once a base camp is established, astronauts might be able to get oxygen from chemical components in lunar rocks.

Sunlight:
The crater has an elevated rim, which is fully lit 240 days a year and in darkness for no longer than two days at a time. The south pole region's nearly constant sunlight could be used to generate electricity.

Radiation protection: The living units could be buried, or covered with sandbags containing lunar dirt, in order to shield them from micrometeorites and the Sun's high-energy radiation.

Shackleton Crater
This is thought to be the best place to locate a base.

Water:
There is only a little water on the Moon, and it's mostly at the poles. Craters have ice buried just below the surface.

Living quarters:
Expandable living units could be ferried to the Moon and assembled in place.

Power: Solar panels could collect sunlight to provide electricity for heating, venting and pumping oxygen and nitrogen for astronauts to breathe.

SCIENCE ON THE MOON

Picture this: a skinny cable rising thousands of miles from the Moon into the sky. At the end of the cable is a station suspended in space – it's a lunar elevator! This might sound like the stuff of science fiction, but engineers and visionaries have been working on this idea for nearly a century.

MINING THE MOON

Why bother to build a lunar elevator? Lunar soil samples brought back by astronauts were found to contain helium-3. This is rare on Earth, but could be used to fuel a new kind of nuclear power plant on our planet in the future.

LUNAR ELEVATOR

If humans set up a base on the Moon, we will need a way to get materials to and from its surface. The Moon has only one-sixth the gravity of Earth, but it still requires a lot of fuel to launch spacecraft off the surface. A lunar elevator could sharply reduce the effort and expense. The main cable would rise from the equator on the near side of the Moon, and terminate a few hundred miles above Earth. Spaceplanes would transfer people and goods from the elevator to Earth's surface and back.

AUGMENTED REALITY

Press the button to move the lunar elevator cars. Try putting your book down on the floor for this one, and see the cable stretch out towards Earth!

Vision of the Future

This illustration shows a lunar elevator taking humans to a space station, where they'd catch a ride back to Earth. The circular object on the Moon's surface is a liquid mirror telescope.

ASTRONOMY ON THE MOON

Even light takes a long time to cover intergalactic distances, so when we see the light of very distant objects, we are actually seeing energy emitted from them a long time ago. From the Moon, a telescope could peer back into the earliest days of the Universe, almost 13.7 billion years ago. Astronomers propose to one day build a liquid mirror telescope at the Moon's south pole.

LIQUID MIRROR TELESCOPE

A liquid mirror telescope could potentially serve the same purpose as a traditional telescope, but at a fraction of the weight and cost . As wide as a football field, its main mirror would be made of liquid. Slowly spinning, it would form a reflecting pool to observe the earliest days of the Universe.

For use in the telescope, researchers are currently testing special liquids that won't freeze even at the very low temperatures found on the Moon.

⊚ Galaxies through Time
This image, taken by the Hubble Space Telescope, shows galaxies through most of the Universe's history. Images like this can't be taken by Earth-bound telescopes, because our atmosphere gets in the way.

WHERE ARE WE NOW?

Humans haven't visited the Moon since 1972, but space has not been abandoned. Thanks to the launch of the International Space Station (ISS), since October 2000 not a day has gone by without a person in space. There is also an increasing number of robots out there, and the orbiting Hubble Space Telescope sends us astonishing new images every day.

UNMANNED MISSIONS

In 1970 Venera 7, a Soviet spacecraft, landed on Venus. It was the first unmanned vehicle to touch down on another planet and transmit data back to Earth. Since then, unmanned vehicles called probes have explored every planet in our solar system. In 2004, two identical rovers landed on Mars. The rover Opportunity continues to transmit data back to scientists on Earth, and in 2012 was joined by Curiosity – see the pages about Robots on Mars.

◎ *Venera 7 Voyage*
This is a capsule that the Soviet Union sent to Venus.

SPACEFARING NATIONS

When the Soviet Union broke up in 1991, the new Russian Federation continued its space programme. The USA and Russia remained the only countries to send humans into space until 2005, when China launched a manned ship. During the past several years, space probes from many nations, including China (shown right), the USA, Japan, and India, have orbited the Moon.

THE INTERNATIONAL SPACE STATION

The ISS has been home to more than 200 people over the years. As a result, we know more about living and working in space than ever before. There are different sections, or modules, for living and working, powered in part by a massive array of solar panels. The ISS houses six crew at a time and is scheduled to stay in space until at least 2020.

SUPER TELESCOPE

The Hubble Space Telescope has been in orbit since 1990. It allows scientists to peer into the depths of the Universe without Earth's atmosphere getting in the way. The telescope is able to see some of the faintest – and oldest – objects in space, allowing scientists to make profound discoveries about the nature of the Universe.

Virgin Galactic's SpaceShipTwo

SPACE TOURISM

Private companies are developing vehicles to carry paying customers into space, and maybe one day even to the Moon and Mars. Virgin Galactic is one of the leading 'space tourism' companies. They are developing craft to carry people into suborbital space, about 62 miles above Earth. Virgin Galactic planes will take off from Spaceport America in New Mexico.

ASTEROIDS

Asteroids are small rocky objects that orbit the Sun. Most do so in the asteroid belt between Mars and Jupiter. But some of them orbit much closer to our planet, and sometimes even crash into it. Will humans visit these near-Earth asteroids? And what can we learn from them?

ITOKAWA

VITAL STATISTICS
Size: 1,770 feet x 960 feet (540 x 295 m) wide
Gravity: 1/100,000 Earth's gravity
Average temperature: – 89F (– 67C)
Distance from the Sun: 115 million miles (249 million km) average

HAYABUSA

Humans haven't been to an asteroid, but we have sent unmanned spacecraft. The Japanese probe Hayabusa landed on asteroid Itokawa in 2005 and sent samples back to Earth. Itokawa is so far from us that radio communications between the craft and mission control took 16 minutes! Hayabusa's mission took seven years from launch to landing back on Earth.

ASTEROIDS AND COMETS

◯ Asteroids
So far, scientists have identified more than 8,000 near-Earth asteroids, ranging from tiny to more than 20 miles (34 km) long! These lonely rocks are remnants from the original debris out of which the planets formed.

◯ Comets
Along with asteroids, comets sometimes orbit the Sun in Earth's neighbourhood. A big difference is that comets release gas and dust as they speed around the Sun.

WHY VISIT AN ASTEROID?

Visiting an asteroid would be good practice for a Mars mission, but are there other reasons for going? We know what asteroids are made of thanks to meteorites (small pieces of asteroids and comets) which have landed on Earth. Many meteorites are rich in valuable metals, so mining asteroids might someday pay off.

The interior of an iron meteorite.

CAN WE DO IT?

Sending human astronauts to near-Earth asteroids is a real possibility. In 2011, US President Barack Obama announced ambitions to send "astronauts to an asteroid for the first time in history". Studying asteroids up close and bringing back samples would help scientists learn about the formation of the solar system.

🔍 *This capsule carried dust from Itokawa back to Earth for scientists to examine.*

AUGMENTED REALITY

Use pinch, swipe, and zoom to spin asteroid Itokawa as it tumbles through space. The biggest challenge for future astronauts landing on one of these rocks will be how to avoid drifting off!

DEATH FROM THE SKIES?

Danger overhead!
Earth has been hit by asteroids before. A giant impact 65 million years ago probably caused the extinction of large dinosaurs. But luckily for us, asteroid impacts are fairly rare. Also, scientists are working on methods to deflect or destroy future threats of this kind.

Every 100 years:
Asteroids wider than 150 feet (50 metres) might hit Earth, causing local damage in the area of the impact.

Every 2,000 years:
Asteroids wider than 500 feet (150 metres) might hit Earth, causing damage equivalent to a volcano or earthquake.

Every 300,000 years:
An asteroid more than one mile (1.6 kilometres) wide might hit Earth, causing widespread devastation.

Every 5 to 10 million years:
An asteroid as big as the one that probably wiped out large dinosaurs 65 million years ago – wider than five miles (10 kilometres) – might crash into us.

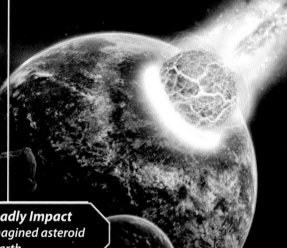

🔍 *Deadly Impact
An imagined asteroid hits Earth.*

THE RED PLANET

MARS

VITAL STATISTICS
38% Earth's gravity
−81F (−63C) average surface temperature
687 days to orbit the Sun
24.7 hours in a day
59% Earth's sunlight
4,221 miles (6,792 km) in diameter, or about
53% that of Earth

DISTANCE FROM THE SUN
141 million miles (227 million km), about 1.5 times as far as Earth
231 years by car at 70 mph (113 km/h)
3 years on Apollo 11

Of all the other planets in our solar system, Mars is the most likely to harbour life. What's more, it's close enough to Earth for humans to be able to get there in a year using currently available technology. A Mars expedition would be a huge, expensive project, but many scientists think the knowledge gained would be worth the effort.

○ **New Spacesuit**
This new kind of pressure suit will wrap the body in tight, stretchy fabric which maintains its pressure even when torn. These new suits would be lighter and more manoeuvrable.

THE ENVIRONMENT ON MARS

Water
There's no liquid water on the surface of Mars. But there are ice caps at the poles. You could melt this ice to drink, or break it down into hydrogen for fuel and oxygen for breathing.

Dust
Massive dust storms on Mars can quickly cover thousands of miles. These tiny particles can get inside spacesuits and damage machinery.

Life
Many scientists think tiny forms of life such as microbes may live on Mars and other planets in our solar system. See the Looking for Life spread for some examples of what might be out there.

O_2 Air
The atmosphere on Mars is so thin you'd need tanks of oxygen to breathe and a spacesuit to make up for the lack of air pressure.

Temperature
It's really, really cold on Mars. The average temperature is −81F (−63C), so any future astronauts will need heated spacesuits.

Radiation
Dangerous ultraviolet light from the Sun irradiates the Martian surface constantly.

○ *Engineer and inventor Dr. Dava Newman wears her new spacesuit.*

○ **The Martian Surface**
In 1965, the Mariner 4 probe sent back the first photos.

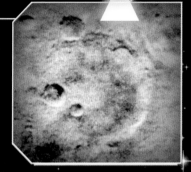

○ **Underground Water?**
The white streak in this 2005 image shows a place where water seems to have recently cut through sand dunes. Is there water underground on Mars?

○ **Dust Storms**
These are a frequent danger on Mars.

READY FOR MARS?

Do you have what it takes to join the first mission to Mars? Answer the following questions, and then score yourself one point for every A, two points for every B, and three points for every C.

1 Your entire life will be strictly timetabled, with work, exercise, and even sleep all planned out in advance. How well can you handle a relentless schedule?
A I need to take breaks
B I can get used to it
C I'm always very organized

2 In space, attention to detail can mean the difference between life and death. Would you panic when your personal safety is on the line?
A I'm already freaking out
B I might drop the ball
C I'm calm under pressure

3 You'll have almost no contact with your family and friends for more than a year. How would you deal with the separation?
A I'd miss them terribly
B They'd be in my thoughts
C They can wait – this is my dream

4 Living in almost no gravity can cause nausea, disorientation, and extreme discomfort. Could you endure motion sickness for months on end?
A I get seasick in the bath
B It would be distracting
C No problem, I'll work through it

5 Even after working for 15 hours, you might have to respond to an emergency. Can you function efficiently when you're tired?
A I really need my rest
B I can do it with lots and lots of sugar
C Important work keeps me focused

6 Astronauts keep clean with dry shampoo and baby wipes. Could you give up baths for over a year?
A I get itchy imagining it
B I'd try not to get dirty
C Think of the time saved

RESULTS:
6 to 8 Grounded
9 to 11 Head in the clouds, feet still on Earth
12 to 14 Almost reached orbit, keep trying
15 to 18 All systems go!

AUGMENTED REALITY

Use pinch, swipe, and zoom to focus on the Red Planet and its moons, Phobos and Deimos. They are thought to be asteroids which were captured by Mars' gravity millions of years ago.

ROBOTS ON MARS

SPIRIT AND OPPORTUNITY

Since the 1970s, only a few spacecraft have reached Mars. However, in 2004 NASA landed two identical rovers, Spirit and Opportunity, on the planet. Their observations showed that the planet was once home to a lot of liquid water. The rovers were only expected to remain active for a year or so, but Spirit continued transmitting data until 2010 and Opportunity was still going strong in 2012.

Before humans can go to the Red Planet, robots have to collect as much data about it as possible. NASA's Curiosity, a one-tonne rover the size of a car, touched down on August 6, 2012 after a journey of almost nine months. Its initial two-year mission is to study the surface of Mars for signs that life may once have dwelt there – and may even still survive underground.

DESTINATION CRATER

Curiosity touched down in Gale Crater. It will spend several years slowly climbing a mountain that rises from the floor of the crater, studying each layer as it goes, to search for ancient signs of life or habitable environments.

⊙ Water Detector
This locates ice underground by shooting neutrons at the ground and detecting water-bearing molecules.

AUGMENTED REALITY

Use the blue ◁⊙▷ ⊙ icons to move Curiosity around, and tap the ⊙ icon to bring up the view from the rover's laser sights. Use the green ◁⊙▷ ⊙ icons to adjust the direction of the beam, and the red ⊙ icon to fire at interesting targets.

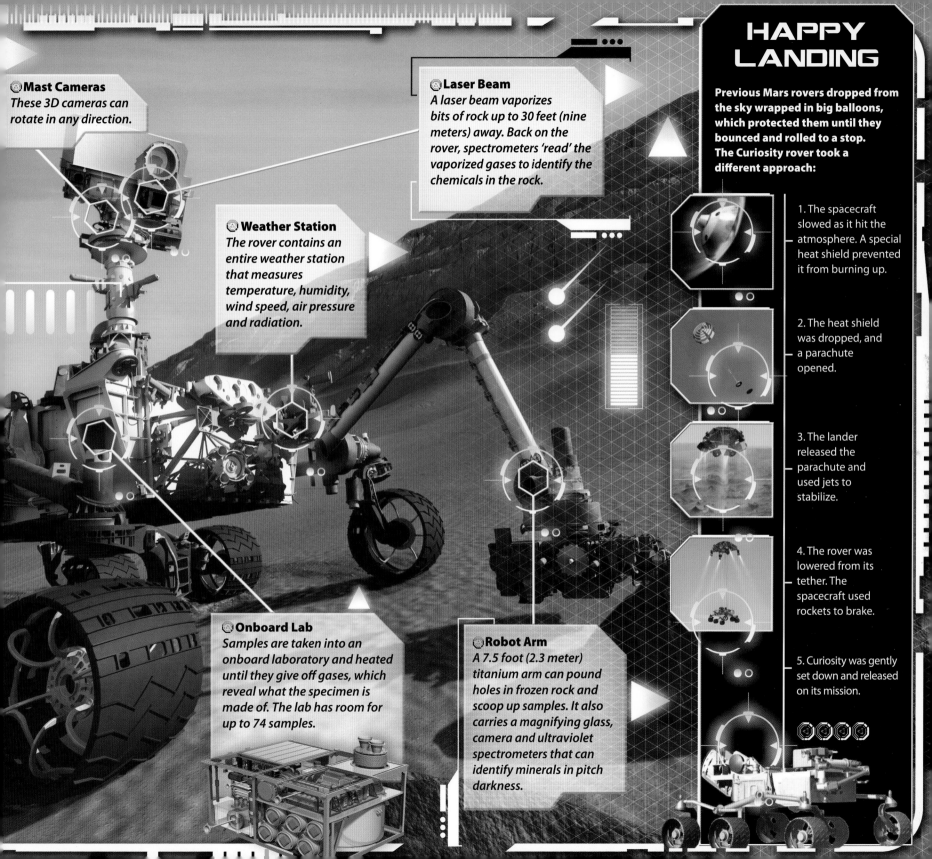

Mast Cameras
These 3D cameras can rotate in any direction.

Laser Beam
A laser beam vaporizes bits of rock up to 30 feet (nine meters) away. Back on the rover, spectrometers 'read' the vaporized gases to identify the chemicals in the rock.

Weather Station
The rover contains an entire weather station that measures temperature, humidity, wind speed, air pressure and radiation.

Onboard Lab
Samples are taken into an onboard laboratory and heated until they give off gases, which reveal what the specimen is made of. The lab has room for up to 74 samples.

Robot Arm
A 7.5 foot (2.3 meter) titanium arm can pound holes in frozen rock and scoop up samples. It also carries a magnifying glass, camera and ultraviolet spectrometers that can identify minerals in pitch darkness.

HAPPY LANDING

Previous Mars rovers dropped from the sky wrapped in big balloons, which protected them until they bounced and rolled to a stop. The Curiosity rover took a different approach:

1. The spacecraft slowed as it hit the atmosphere. A special heat shield prevented it from burning up.

2. The heat shield was dropped, and a parachute opened.

3. The lander released the parachute and used jets to stabilize.

4. The rover was lowered from its tether. The spacecraft used rockets to brake.

5. Curiosity was gently set down and released on its mission.

JOURNEY TO MARS

Can people really go to Mars? Why not? We've already sent people to the Moon and back. A Mars voyage would take much longer but might be possible in a spaceship like the Nautilus X, a craft imagined by NASA engineers to start from an orbiting space station and use detachable vehicles to land.

Engine
A spacecraft like this one would likely use a new type of ion drive engine.

No Streamlining
Streamlining is only needed to help a spacecraft slice through the air in a planet's atmosphere. Since the Nautilus X will be launched from a space station, it doesn't need to be streamlined.

HOW LONG WOULD THE JOURNEY TAKE?

It would take six to nine months in a conventional spaceship. These use a burst of energy to escape Earth's orbit, but then simply coast the rest of the way. Scientists are currently working on 'ion drive' technology, which would shorten the trip dramatically by providing constant acceleration.

Solar Panels
Huge arrays of solar panels would capture energy from the Sun to power the spacecraft.

AUGMENTED REALITY

NASA is working on different versions of the Nautilus, but they all have a thin spine with 'arms'. The solar panels provide vital energy for the flight, and don't slow the ship down because there is no friction in a vacuum.

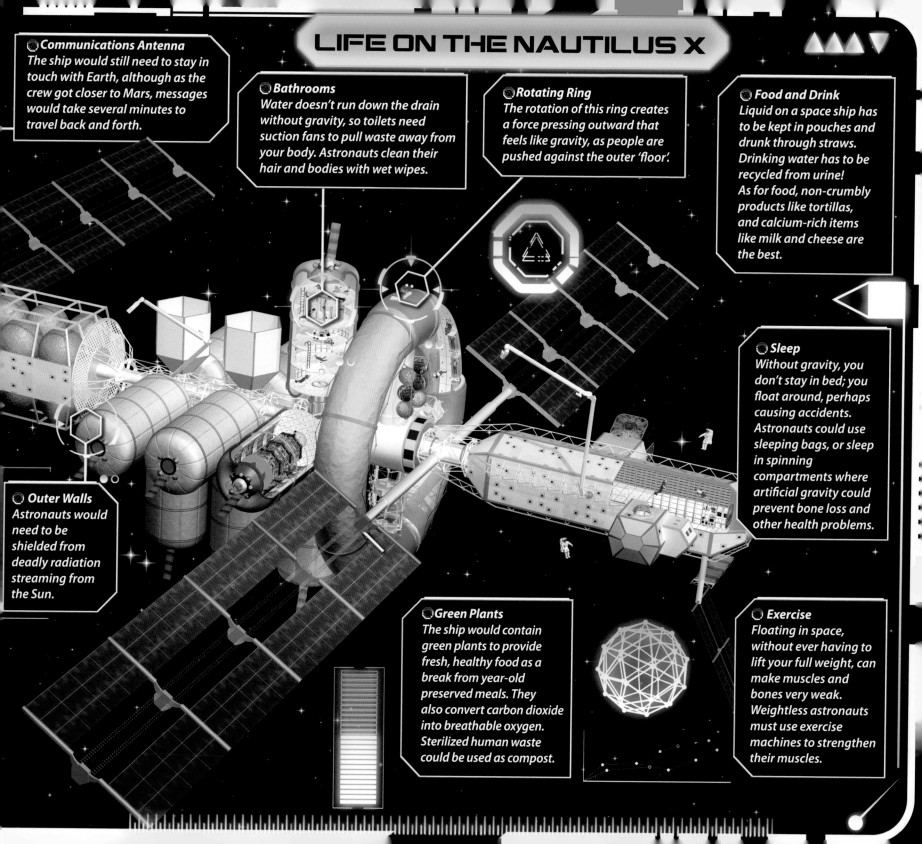

Communications Antenna
The ship would still need to stay in touch with Earth, although as the crew got closer to Mars, messages would take several minutes to travel back and forth.

Bathrooms
Water doesn't run down the drain without gravity, so toilets need suction fans to pull waste away from your body. Astronauts clean their hair and bodies with wet wipes.

Rotating Ring
The rotation of this ring creates a force pressing outward that feels like gravity, as people are pushed against the outer 'floor'.

Food and Drink
Liquid on a space ship has to be kept in pouches and drunk through straws. Drinking water has to be recycled from urine! As for food, non-crumbly products like tortillas, and calcium-rich items like milk and cheese are the best.

Sleep
Without gravity, you don't stay in bed; you float around, perhaps causing accidents. Astronauts could use sleeping bags, or sleep in spinning compartments where artificial gravity could prevent bone loss and other health problems.

Outer Walls
Astronauts would need to be shielded from deadly radiation streaming from the Sun.

Green Plants
The ship would contain green plants to provide fresh, healthy food as a break from year-old preserved meals. They also convert carbon dioxide into breathable oxygen. Sterilized human waste could be used as compost.

Exercise
Floating in space, without ever having to lift your full weight, can make muscles and bones very weak. Weightless astronauts must use exercise machines to strengthen their muscles.

TERRAFORMING MARS

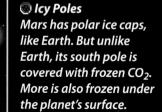

Today, the surface of Mars is barren. But the ingredients for a fertile environment are all there, frozen underground. Could we release them, and bring Mars to life by terraforming, making it more Earthlike, and so habitable for humans? Some scientists think so. But it could cost trillions of pounds and may take thousands of years.

◎ Icy Poles
Mars has polar ice caps, like Earth. But unlike Earth, its south pole is covered with frozen CO_2. More is also frozen under the planet's surface.

1 ADD HEAT

Mars is currently so cold that even the gases in the air can freeze. The first step in making the planet habitable would be warming the poles to release frozen water and carbon dioxide (CO_2), one of the so-called greenhouse gases that keep Earth warm. There are a number of ways to do this:

◎ Massive Explosions
Asteroids could be steered toward Mars, creating giant impacts. This would release CO_2 and water into the atmosphere.

◎ Giant Mirrors
Giant mirrors in orbit could focus sunlight on the poles, returning frozen CO_2 and water to the atmosphere.

◎ Darken the Surface
Dark colours absorb sunlight. Covering the Martian surface with dust would speed up the warming process.

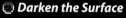

2 CREATE A GREENHOUSE EFFECT

As frozen carbon dioxide turned to gas and entered the Martian atmosphere, it would trap heat. Factories would produce and release other powerful greenhouse gases. Increased warming would in turn release yet more frozen gas and so on, until temperatures were high enough to melt ice.

◎ AFTER ONE YEAR
The Martian surface is dry, reddish rock. There is no surface water, except for ice at the poles.

◎ AFTER 10 YEARS
The rocks are now covered by bacteria, lichens and algae. There are patches of snow on the surface. The sky is paler and clearer but stil reddish.

3 ADD LIFE

Life would be introduced in stages. Some microbes could be brought in at once, to begin building soil and enriching the atmosphere. Other life forms would follow as the atmosphere warmed and thickened.

4 ADD WATER

When the atmosphere warmed enough, vast stores of ice locked underground would melt and evaporate. Water that entered the atmosphere would come back to the surface as snow and rain. Mars may have enough water frozen underground to eventually produce rivers and oceans.

AFTER 1,000 YEARS
Oceans expand, and life thrives in the oxygen-rich atmosphere. Mountaintops and polar regions remain frozen.

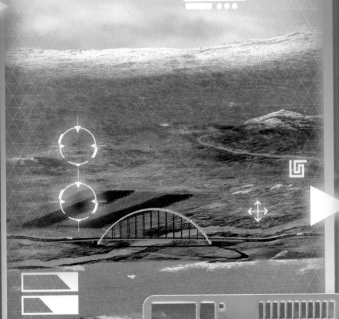

AFTER 100 YEARS
Lakes and oceans form, as underground ice melts and enters the atmosphere to form clouds and rain. Plants and topsoil abound.

AUGMENTED REALITY

Use the toggle to fly the plane over the Martian landscape. A lightweight plane like this one could survey the terrain as preparation for a terraforming project.

THE OUTER SOLAR SYSTEM

The planets beyond Mars are huge, low-density bodies known as gas giants. These enormous worlds are some of the most mysterious places in our solar system.

Jupiter

SUPERSIZE PLANETS

Jupiter is by far the largest planet in our region of space. Comets which might threaten Earth are attracted by its gravity and thrown towards the Sun or the edges of the solar system.

AUGMENTED REALITY

Jupiter holds the record for the planet with the most moons: 64 have been discovered so far. The animation shows Jupiter with Io, Europa, Ganymede, and Callisto, the four moons discovered by the early astronomer Galileo.

WHAT'S OUT THERE?

On Earth, life requires water. But what if life elsewhere evolved from a different set of chemicals? Could aliens live in molten sulphur, drawing energy from the volcanoes on Jupiter's moon Io? Could life swim in the hydrocarbon lakes on Saturn's moon Titan?

○ **Saturn's Rings**
These have been known almost since the invention of the telescope. They are made up of ice particles and rock dust.

THE FURTHEST WORLDS

Uranus and Neptune have only ever been visited by one spacecraft: the probe Voyager 2. On Uranus, it found evidence of an ocean of boiling water, as well as 10 new moons. The probe later passed just 3,106 miles (5,000 km) from the cloud tops of Neptune, and discovered five moons plus the Great Dark Spot, a huge storm. Images from the Hubble Space Telescope show that the spot has since vanished, but other, smaller spots have formed. Voyager 2 found evidence that Neptune's largest moon, Triton, is the coldest object visited in the solar system. It has a 'volcano' of nitrogen ice on its surface!

Saturn

Uranus

Neptune

○ **Marvellous Moons**
Saturn also has some amazing moons, such as Enceladus. NASA's Cassini probe discovered vapour jets erupting from its surface. If the moon contains heated liquid, life may be found there.

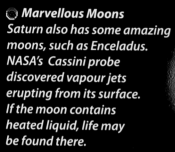

DISTANT TRAVELLERS

1972: Pioneer 10 (mission to Jupiter) and Pioneer 11 (mission to Saturn, left) were the first probes to cross the asteroid belt lying between Mars and Jupiter. Both spacecraft eventually left the solar system, and continue to travel deeper into space.

1977: American spacecraft Voyagers 1 and 2 headed to Jupiter and Saturn. Voyager 2 (below) then visited Uranus and Neptune. The two probes are now travelling billions of miles from the Sun, analysing interstellar space.

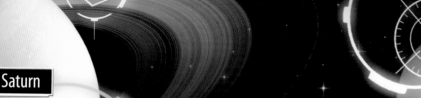

LOOKING FOR LIFE

Energy for Life
Jupiter's moon Io has over 400 volcanoes, making it the most geologically active place in the solar system. Could this energy fuel alien life?

Jupiter, Saturn, Uranus and Neptune have more than 160 moons between them. Europa, one of Jupiter's largest moons, is especially intriguing because there is a saltwater ocean beneath its icy surface. On Earth, life exists wherever there is water. Future missions to Europa may reveal whether the same is true on this remote moon.

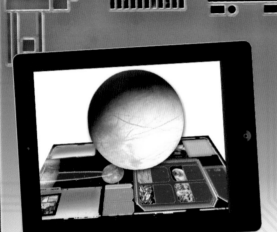

AUGMENTED REALITY

Use pinch, swipe, and zoom to explore Europa, one of Jupiter's most interesting moons. Could there be life in the salty oceans beneath the satellite's icy surface?

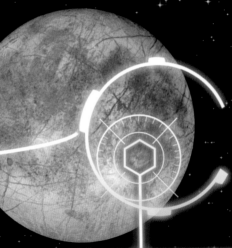

EUROPA

VITAL STATISTICS

14% Earth's gravity
– 260F (– 162C) average surface temperature
84 hours in a day
3.7% Earth's sunlight
1,940 miles (3,122 km) in diameter, about tha
Earth's Moon

DISTANCE FROM THE SU

483 million miles (778 million km) average
789 years by car at 70 mph (113 km/h)
9 years on Apollo 11
6.5 days by ion drive with constant 1g acceleration (future technology)

EXTREMOPHILES

The surface of Mars and the oceans of Europa are both extreme environments. Yet many organisms have adapted to conditions almost as harsh here on Earth. The discovery of these 'extremophiles' has raised hopes that the extreme environments on Mars and Europa might be habitable after all.

UNDERWATER ROBOT

Engineers at Stone Aerospace in Texas are developing a robot that can navigate on its own in the ocean under the ice of Antarctica. Someday they hope to send a version aboard a spacecraft to Europa. There, a nuclear-powered generator on board would melt through miles of ice to get at the ocean underneath. Then instruments could measure the chemistry and composition of the water, and perhaps discover life.

EARTH'S TOUGHEST SURVIVORS

If microbes can survive in Earth's harshest environments, why not on other planets?

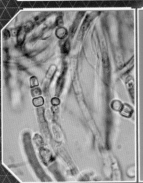

Cyanobacteria
Can survive: Extreme cold and dryness. Some species have survived eight million years inside solid ice!
Lives in: Antarctic ice
Similar habitat: Surface of Mars

Nematode worm
Can survive: Total lack of sunlight and plant-based food
Lives in: Mile-deep rocks 1.3 kilometres (0.8 miles) underground
Similar habitat: Below the surface on Mars

Tubeworms
Can survive: Total darkness, toxic chemicals
Lives in: Volcanic vents in the ocean floor, feeding on chemical energy
Similar habitat: Oceans of Europa

Bacteria
Can survive: Deadly radiation, cold, dehydration, acid, vacuum
Lives in: Cooling ponds of nuclear reactors. Can survive a radiation dose 5,000 times larger than the amount needed to kill a human
Similar habitat: Martian surface

WHAT DOES LIFE NEED?

Most known planets are too hot or too cold for life as we know it. But some planets have been found with temperatures that would support liquid water and perhaps life. Others might have life forms that don't need liquid water at all.

BEYOND OUR SOLAR SYSTEM

All the planets, moons and asteroids we've explored so far orbit the same star – our Sun. But the Sun is just one of 200 to 400 billion stars in the giant group that makes up the Milky Way galaxy.

THE MILKY WAY

Look up in the sky on a very dark night and you will see a big, fuzzy band of light spanning the sky. That glow is actually from billions of stars, too distant to distinguish individually, but all part of the Milky Way.

Our galaxy is so immense that it takes light 100,000 years to cross from one side to the other. Plenty of room to explore!

⊙ The Earliest Days of the Universe
This photo was made by combining Hubble Space Telescope data taken over a ten-year period. It shows the most faraway galaxies ever observed. They formed about 13.2 billion years ago, soon after the Big Bang.

BILLIONS OF EXOPLANETS?

'Exoplanet' is the term for a planet outside our solar system. Thousands of stars have already been found to have exoplanets, and the search has barely begun. There are likely to be billions more. Scientists are already focusing on the question of whether any of these planets support life.

⊙ Our Beautiful Home
The Milky Way is a spiral, like the Messier 51 galaxy (left). We can't see the shape of the Milky Way directly, because we're inside it.

OKU

Orthopaedic Knowledge Update:

Shoulder and Elbow

3

WITHDRAWN

B43